How to Make Sock Puppets

by Aileen Weintraub

Illustrated by Michael Rex

MONDO

Sock puppets are fun to make.

Come and see how to make boy puppets and girl puppets, and cat puppets, too.

What You Need

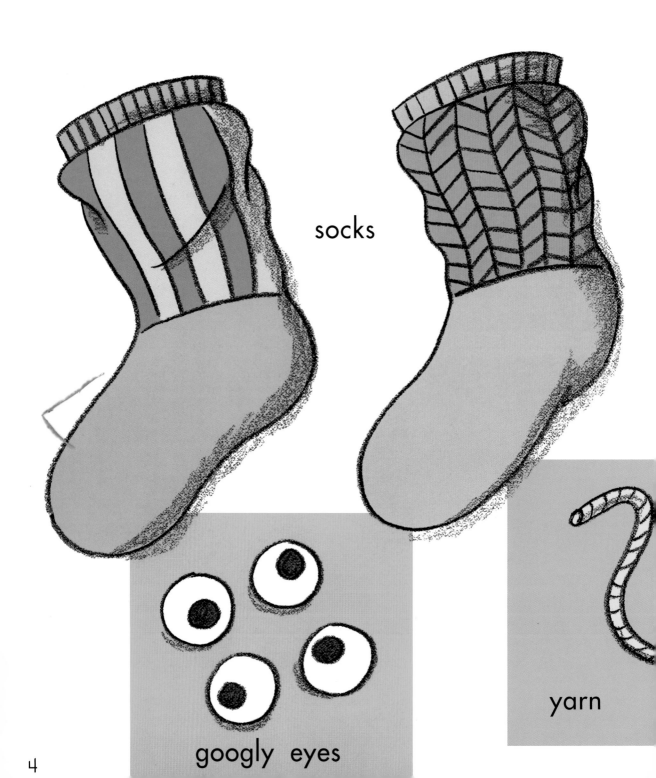

socks

googly eyes

yarn

glue

scissors

black paper

red paper

gray paper

5

Make a Boy or a Girl Puppet

Put a sock on the table.
Lay the open end of the sock
away from you.

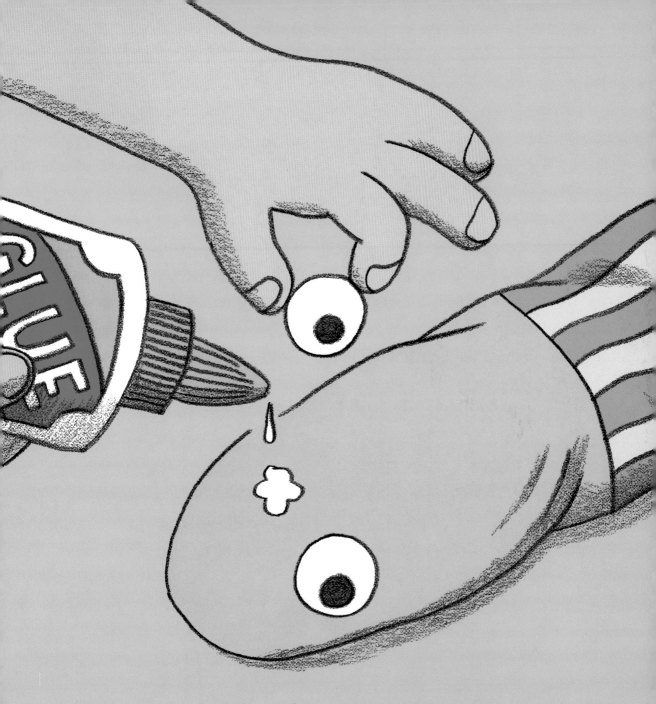

Glue two googly eyes on the sock,
up a little from the toe.

Cut out the puppet's nose
from the black paper.

Glue the nose under the eyes.

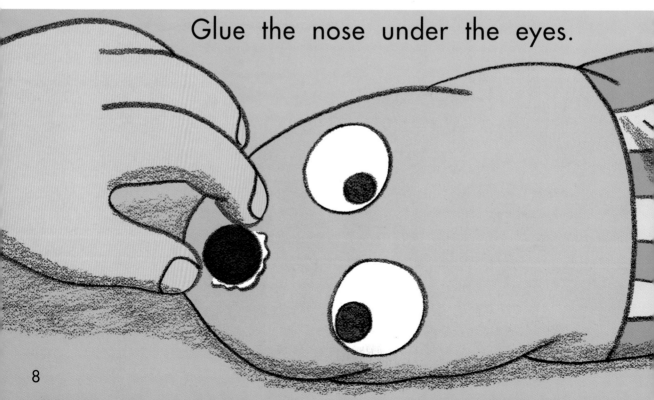

Cut out the puppet's mouth from the red paper.

Put your hand in the sock.

Open and close your thumb and fingers to see where the mouth will go.

ull the sock off
f your hand.

lue the mouth
n the puppet.

Cut the yarn to make
hair for the puppet.

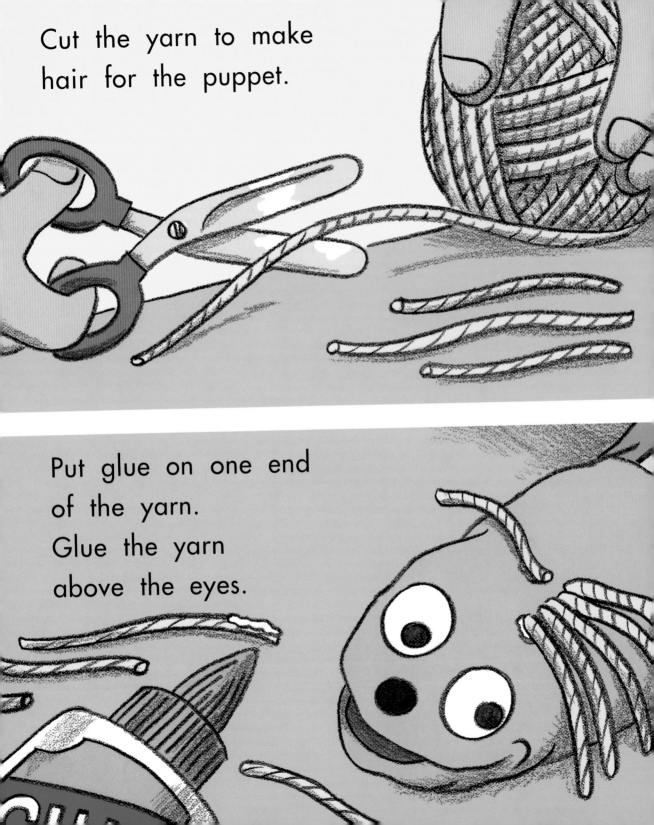

Put glue on one end
of the yarn.
Glue the yarn
above the eyes.

Now, make a girl puppet the same way.
Add a hat, glasses, or scarf just for fun!

Make a Cat Puppet

Cut out a gray S for the tail. Cut out three gray triangles for the ears and nose.

Cut out long strips from the black paper for whiskers.

Cut out a red mouth.
Glue the tail, ears,
nose, whiskers, and mouth
on to the puppet.
Glue on two googly eyes.

Now, put on a puppet show!